SMOOTH SAILING TO VENTURE CAPITAL FUNDING

A Real World Guide For Entrepreneurs And Investors

Ronald J. Carlini
Therese Carlini Moss

First Edition

Published by Venture Capital Strategies
San Jose California

Smooth Sailing to Venture Capital Funding
Copyright © 2004 by Ronald J. Carlini

Published by
Venture Capital Strategies
1685 Branham Lane Suite 270
San Jose, California 95118, USA

ISBN 0-9760908-5-6

LCCN 2004111879

Printed in the USA
October 2004

*To
Bernadette
and
Natalie*

Acknowledgements
Diane, Ben, Steven, Christa & Christiana

*Special acknowledgement to
Bob Moss whose outstanding efforts and support
are deeply appreciated.*

Introduction from the Old Salt

Ahoy There! Are you planning to raise funds to support your business? Many Entrepreneurs seek Venture Capital Funding for their start-up or early phase companies, and quickly realize that it's not as easy as it sounds. They follow all of the guidelines on 'how to write a business plan' and go to scores of seminars on 'the business model.' They think they have everything they need in place to approach the financial community. Some of them never realize that they weren't ever really ready.

Interestingly, many VC's never give a hard "no" or they say "no" without giving any clue as to why they are not going to invest. Sometimes they give encouragement, like "good product idea" without having any intention of investing. Vague praise is even worse than a negative response because it results in false hope. Of course, all of this leaves founders and entrepreneurs confused and frustrated. Why wouldn't it?

Why does this happen? In working with a large number of companies over the years, I have found that people who started companies did not fully appreciate, nor really understand, all of the fundamental elements that are core to the fund raising process. No matter what level of business experience the founders had, some key areas were always missed. I have worked with first *time entrepreneurs, seasoned investors, and previously successful CEO's, and they all needed some level of assistance and guidance to successfully raise investment funds.*

Although there are many books and articles available on the subject, I could not find a single source that presented the "critical mass" of information needed in an easy to read and easy to understand format.

This book focuses on teaching companies to evaluate the fundamentals of their own business model and to measure them against what the financial community is currently funding. You will learn how to identify and then leverage your company's strengths and to neutralize or eliminate the weaknesses.   You will learn to optimize your business model both to attract investors and to build a strong and profitable company. This book provides the information every company needs to successfully approach the investment community.

The underlying concept is that there is a specific set of obstacles that you must overcome, to qualify your company in the eyes of the investment community. For the first time, this book identifies these obstacles and tells you how to successfully deal with them.

Our goal is to provide very useful "real world" information in a way that is easy to read and to understand. Our hope is that this will make your journey more pleasant and more successful.

SMOOTH SAILING
TO VENTURE CAPITAL FUNDING

PART 1: Preparing to Set Sail

PART 2: Charting the Course

PART 3: Drawing the Map to VC Funding Island

PART 4: Choosing Your Destination

PART 5: Setting Sail is Setting "Sale"

PART 6: Key to the Treasure Chest

PART 7: Walking the Plank

PART 8: You Have Arrived!

PART 9: Ship's Log

Part 1
Preparing To Set Sail

Starting Out on the Adventure

This book helps new entrepreneurs and investors understand the very basic concepts involved in raising venture capital.

Using the sailing analogy, we will describe planning the route to travel, creating the all important treasure map, and following it to your ultimate destination: VC Funding Island. We'll show you how to navigate to avoid the dangerous pitfalls, like icebergs and bad weather, and how to beat the pirates who are your competition.

So you have valuable cargo: a great product idea or new service. You may even have done some significant product development. There is still a lot of sailing ahead to steer your new company boat through the sea of the marketplace to discover its treasures. You will need the gold coins of Venture Capital from investors. But there are a lot of pirates competing for those coins, so watch out. Let's get started by understanding what Venture Capital is, who has it, and what we need to do to get it.

The Treasure: What is Venture Capital?

Start-up companies and newer companies need funds to implement their business models and to grow their business. Venture Capital firms provide the majority of these funds. A Venture Capital firm usually consists of a series of individual funds, each of which has general partners (VC's) and limited partners (investors).

A Venture Capital Fund is formed as a limited partnership in which the general partners select start-ups and early stage companies to invest in. Which specific markets the funds will invest in are determined at the time the fund is formed. The money invested is raised from limited partners. The partnership has a limited timeframe of five to seven years. When the time of the partnership runs out, the proceeds of the investments are divided among the general and limited partners.

Venture Capitalists are willing to assume the risks associated with new companies in exchange for equity (shares of ownership – also known as "stock") in the company. Their challenge is to invest in companies that will grow rapidly and become highly profitable in a relatively short amount of time. Their objective is to make money.

__From The Old Salt's Journal__
I once asked a prominent Venture Capitalist in Silicon Valley, how he judged his own performance? His answer was that he truly enjoyed working with entrepreneurs in building new companies, but "how much money he made" was the only way to keep score. He went on to say that good product ideas are easy; making a lot of money with them is hard to do.

The Venture Capitalist must be totally convinced that you and your company have a greater chance to be successful than other companies seeking funds.

Who has the Coins?

Raising money is a difficult process even in the best of times. The events of the past few years have made the task even harder.

The Economy
> High tech bubble burst in early 2000
> Still sluggish and slow to recover

Corporate Scandals
> Enron, WorldCom, etc. etc. etc.
> FASB, Sarbanes-Oxley

There was a shift in the momentum of venture funding, swinging back to the use of relatively conservative investment qualification measures.

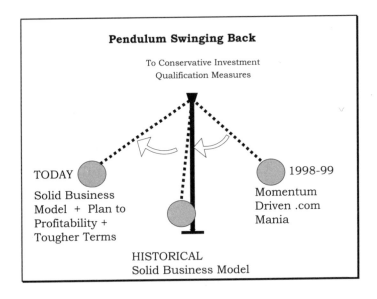

The result is that we are now emerging from a period in which VC investments were at a four-year low. Over the past several years, some very large VC firms have actually returned some of the monies raised back to their investors. In 2002, seven VC firms returned a staggering 2.7 billion dollars due to a lack of what they termed, "good investment opportunities." The good news is that there are 1664 VC firms and still plenty of money available, some 60 to 80 billion dollars, for the companies that have solid business models and know how to navigate though the fund-raising waters.

There's more good news in that the labor market is rich with highly skilled and experienced people looking for the right start-up opportunity. Many others are sitting in hold positions waiting and looking for that next great new company. In addition, larger companies often have corporate investment funds available and are anxious to work with new ventures that complement their business growth strategies.

Now may be the best of times for you to start a company.

Where to Get Coins

"Investors" come in many shapes and sizes. There are many ways to raise funds to get your project started and to keep it going.   There is risk associated with any investment, but there is also great potential reward.

From The Old Salt's Journal

It is not uncommon for founders to risk all they have. A long time ago, when I was house hunting, I asked a couple why they were selling their home. They said they needed the money to invest in a new franchise. I thought they were foolish to be so personally committed to a new company – especially one that sold hamburgers! Yes – it was McDonalds.

Let's look at some possible sources for coins:

⚓ Your Own Money

You will have to invest in your company. If you aren't willing to take the personal risk and invest your savings and borrowings, why should VC's?

⚓ Friends and Family

If you are totally committed and convinced your endeavor is worth the risk in terms of high potential gains, then they are a source of funds. Make sure they are well aware of, and prepared for, the possibility of losing their investment. The results, both good and bad, will affect these relationships for years to come.

⚓ Angel Investors

Angel Investors are individuals who have some amount of personal wealth and invest in start-ups. They are, in many cases, the first source of outside funding. By some estimates, there are hundreds of thousands of angel investors who have invested billions of dollars. Angels invest in the very early stages, and usually on reasonable terms, so they are an excellent source of start-up funds. Although there are many more Angels than VC's, the last several years of downturn in the market have been very hard on Angels, with many investments being washed out. They are now beginning to invest again, and many Angel groups can be found on the Internet. Here are just a few examples:

Alliance of Angels (Seattle)
http://www.allianceofangels.com/

Angel Organization Summit's Angel Directory
(Regional and National Directory)
http://angelsummit.org/

AngelDeals.com (online fee-based resource)
http://www.angeldeals.com/

Atlanta Technology Angels (Atlanta)
http://www.angelatlanta.com/

Band of Angels (Silicon Valley)
http://www.bandangels.com/

Tech Coast Angels (Southern California)
http://www.techcoastangels.com/

⚓ Corporations

Many large public corporations have their own investment funds or invest in VC funds that specialize in their industry. They are interested in making money on their investment and, equally (or more) important, in gaining access to new technology that complements their core business. They usually take a minority position of less than 10 percent of the company and many of them will not invest unless there is a lead Venture Capital firm. There is a word or two of caution when working with large corporations. The terms they demand may be more limiting than those from a VC firm. They also may steer the product more specifically toward their own requirements. That being said, your objective is to get funded and corporate backing is a feasible consideration. Check the web sites of firms that you think might be interested in your products.

These are all viable options to pursue for funding before you approach VC firms. They will provide the initial coins you need to assemble your core management team, develop and tweak your business model, begin product development, and start prospecting to potential customers. All of which positions your company to set sail for VC Funding Island.

To have smooth sailing, you will need to avoid a number of treacherous obstacles that could sink your boat. No matter what the source of initial funding, in order to get the boat launched from the dock, you will have to avoid the first obstacle: the Sandbar of Commitment.

> ## Obstacle #1
> ## Insufficient Personal Commitment in terms of Time, Money, and Dedication

If you are not totally committed to your project and don't have your "own skin in it", why should the investors take the risk? They know that building a successful company will at times be rough sailing, and they need to know you are willing to weather the storms and not abandon ship at the first sign of trouble.

Avoiding Obstacles: TACK and JIBE

When navigating uncharted waters, it may be necessary to adjust your course to avoid obstacles. For each obstacle, we will recommend actions that will help keep it from sinking your boat.

The Nautical Terms "Tack" and "Jibe" (a.k.a. Gybe) are actions that a captain takes to change the course of the ship. The captain uses the wind to keep the boat going in the desired direction – rather than letting the environment determine the direction.

In our context, these terms will describe actions you can take to correct your course, in order to avoid obstacles and keep your ship heading in the desired direction.

TACK & JIBE

In the case of Obstacle #1: The Sandbar of Commitment, you can navigate around this obstacle by showing that you have invested your own money from savings or borrowings and that you are spending full time on building the company, perhaps having given up a secure and comfortable job.

**For Smooth Sailing
Past Obstacle #1**

**Make The Personal
Commitment in
Time, Money, and
Dedication**

PART 2
Charting the Course

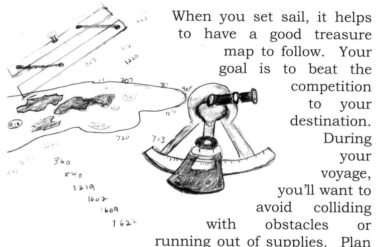

When you set sail, it helps to have a good treasure map to follow. Your goal is to beat the competition to your destination. During your voyage, you'll want to avoid colliding with obstacles or running out of supplies. Plan your journey and create your map before you leave the dock. You would be surprised how many start-ups end up at the bottom of the sea because their treasure map was flawed.

An exceptional map is made up of four pieces:

⚓ **Qualified People**

⚓ **Large Market Potential**

⚓ **Superior Product/Services**

⚓ **Solid Financials**

If any sector is weak, the map may be useless. The weaker the map, the less likely you'll ever reach your destination.

CREW: QUALIFIED PEOPLE

Before you can set sail, you need a strong and experienced crew. Having a good product or service idea is not enough. The bottom of the sea of Silicon Valley is filled with boats loaded with good products, sunk by failing to avoid major obstacles. The investors know that a treasure map is of little value if the captain and crew cannot follow it. That is, if they cannot successfully execute the business plan.

One veteran entrepreneur who has helped to fund several startups tells us, "The Crew is the most important consideration to many VC's. I have often been told that an 'A' crew with a 'B' product is more fundable than a 'B' crew with an 'A' product."

An experienced crew is highly desirable because they have shown they can navigate these waters and investors don't want to pay for "on the job training" that might include hitting a few costly obstacles and possibly sinking the boat.   They also have the mindset and skills that are more suited for the small company, start-up environment.   They are not afraid to take risks, are self-motivated, and can do the work themselves, without a lot of staff support.

From The Old Salt's Journal

Early in my career, I was in a staff position, along with several thousand others, at IBM's Data Processing Headquarters in White Plains, N.Y.   I was assigned with 15 others, to form a new company, Satellite Business Systems (SBS).   We were relocated to a small office complex and all support functions were cut off.   Most of us managed to adjust to the new working environment, except Jack.   He could not function without the staff support that is part of the large company environment.   One day, Jack was reviewing his work assignment and asked me whom he could call for support.   I suggested he call his mom, other than her, he was on his own and would have to do the assignment all by himself.   Within 30 days, Jack requested, and was granted a transfer back to his old staff position at IBM.   Jack clearly did not have the mindset for a startup environment.

**Obstacle #2
Lack of Experienced Management**

TACK & JIBE

The initial crew of an early stage startup is usually a small group of founding entrepreneurs. The key founder may become the Chief Executive Officer (CEO and captain of the boat). The other key crewmember is the Chief Technical Officer (CTO), who may also wear the Vice President of Engineering hat, and is responsible for the product design and development. When first starting out, most companies use outside services or a part time controller for the financial and accounting functions.

As the company matures, individuals with the required sets of skills are added to expand the management team.

Additional Crewmembers:

⚓ Chief Financial Officer (CFO), who takes care of the money, is added when the company is actively producing products and generating revenues.

⚓ Vice President of Sales and Marketing, who prospects for early customer commitments and forms strategic alliances, is added when the product is ready for field test and evaluations.

⚓ Vice President of Manufacturing is added when the initial product development is completed and there are initial customer orders.

From The Old Salt's Journal
*One word of caution is not to ramp up the sales
staff, the manufacturing staff and the facilities
too early. I have seen several cases where the
sales and manufacturing functions were ramped
up before product development was completed.
The result was the sales people had nothing to
sell and the manufacturing people had nothing to
make. With no revenues, the cash was burned at
a high rate and the companies were in serious
trouble.*

There are many highly qualified people available to
fill these positions. They will be able to assess your
company's potential and assist you with their
network of contacts. The VC's also can be a source of
crewmembers. Many VC firms have a pool of skilled
people who are referred to as "executives in waiting."
Founders should not be concerned that more
experienced people are being added to the
management team because there will be many
positions to fill as the company grows. Initially
everyone will be asked to wear many hats.

**For Smooth Sailing
Past Obstacle #2**

**Hire Experienced Managers
with Solid Credentials**

Captain CEO

The most important member of the crew is "Captain CEO." The captain has the vision to look far out and see where to steer the boat, often through rough waters. To do so, requires specific experience:

⚓ **Solid Set of Credentials**   Executive Management positions within your particular Industry Segment

⚓ **Operating Experience**   General Management with profit and loss responsibilities

⚓ **Successful Track Record**   CEO of a successful start-up

Successful CEO's possess outstanding leadership qualities that enable them to lead by example with passion, commitment, vision, and dedication. The CEO must be able to attract, hire, retain, and motivate talented people for the crew positions. Exceptional CEO's are open to suggestions as team builders and active players. They have strong communication skills both inside and outside of the company. One very key attribute: CEO's are always working with a "sense of urgency." Their attitudes and ethics are contagious and invigorating.

The CEO must work well with the Board of Directors and with funding VC's. The CEO will be in a highly exposed position, and needs to be able to adapt to being mentored and coached. The smart CEO will take advantage of the skills and the experience of the board members and VC's.

Not all founders make good CEO's. Some do not possess the necessary people skills and may be hard-line or inflexible in their attitude and manner of management. Founders must be willing to recognize their  management shortcomings and be willing to accept and work with a qualified CEO. This may sound easy, but some founders suffer from "founderitous" and treat the company as the most important thing in their personal being. They will see the company fail before letting others have a major role in running it.

**Obstacle #3
A Weak or Inexperienced CEO**

TACK & JIBE

The VC's and board members can help find a qualified CEO. Working your network of industry contacts can lead to good candidates. If necessary, the lead founder can assume a different role.

From The Old Salt's Journal

In one very successful start-up I worked with, the founder became the Chief Technical Officer. With his academic credentials, he was able to position the company as a leading edge technology driven enterprise. In another extremely profitable venture, the founder took the role of President for himself. He hired a very experienced CEO. They worked well together as a team. In three years, they built a series of strategic business alliances that produced solid revenues and made the company a highly attractive acquisition candidate.

**For Smooth Sailing
Past Obstacle #3**

**Find a Strong CEO who VC's
can Work with and is
Adaptable and Flexible**

Fleet Admirals: The Board of Directors

You should recruit board members that can be of significant help during the early start-up phase.

They should bring a mix of experience and skills to the company. You want people who:

⚓ Spend whatever time is required in support of the company

⚓ Have a range of skills that compliment the skill set of the management team

⚓ Openly share their ideas and mentor members of the management team

⚓ Demonstrate total support and agreement with the CEO's vision

⚓ Use their industry relationships to promote the company

⚓ Get along together and have positive attitudes

⚓ Monitor the progress of the company and recommend changes in course when necessary

Most startup boards consist of two company officers, two investor representatives, and one independent outsider, who can freely contribute their expertise and experience. Having one or more independent board members is important to help in avoiding deadlocks.

It is best to create an "independent board" as is required under new CEO and Board accountability laws for public companies.

(Note: Any company that goes public will have to conform to The Sarbanes-Oxley Act of 2002: a public company accounting reform and corporate governance guideline. These guidelines include the requirement for an independent board.)

Board members of start-ups usually are compensated with stock options and little or no cash. Good board members are well worth a small equity position and will return the investment many times over in building the future value of the company.

Extra Hands On Deck - Business Services

Two types of services you will need are accounting and legal. Many start-ups make the mistake of trying to save money by doing their own accounting and writing their own legal agreements with little or no professional help. In the long run, this can turn out to be a "penny wise, pound foolish" decision.

There are many good, small to medium size accounting firms with "priceless experience" in working with start-ups. They are preferred over the big accounting firms because they are usually more flexible in adapting to the needs of start-ups. They may be willing to defer or discount their fees. Accounting firms seldom take an equity position, as they must be totally unbiased in auditing the financials of the company. They can save you loads of time and aggravation in setting up accounting procedures, lines of credit, stock options, and employee incentive compensation plans. Accountants are also an excellent source of networking within the industry.

From The Old Salt's Journal
I can tell you from personal experience, having the right lawyer can have a lot to do with the level of success of your business. For example, a startup company that had very little cash on hand, tried to save in legal fees by writing their own joint development agreements and having an experienced, but low cost attorney review them. When they attempted to raise more funds to support their growth, they had a difficult time because it was not clear how much of their technology they still owned. The agreements were restructured and the company had to give up a significant portion of their intellectual property in order to stay in business.

Lawyers live and die by their reputations. Attracting a law firm that has strong ties to the VC community can help open doors and give you an edge over your competitors. A good firm will analyze your business model and it will be a good sign if they agree to work with you. Some law firms have established a venture fund and may take a minor equity position in the company. In this case, they must be careful that they are not so influenced by their investment that it clouds their legal advice and opinions to the company. Lawyers will be invaluable in the process of negotiating investment terms with investors and in entering business alliances and joint development agreements.

If your product ideas can be patented, you will need a patent attorney to correctly file patent applications. You must properly protect your intellectual property rights because they add very significant and tangible value to your company as you develop your products. Also, VC's consider intellectual property to be a "barrier to market entry" for your competition. (We'll discuss the benefits of "barrier to entry" a little later)

From The Old Salt's Journal

I have seen cases where hundreds of millions of dollars were involved and riding on how well the general attorneys and the patent attorneys did their jobs.

For example, ABSea Company used a good patent attorney to file their patent applications and an experienced high tech attorney for their joint development agreements. Competitors tried to challenge the validity of the patents and the rights ABSea Company gained under the development agreements, by filing lawsuits totaling over $300 million. Those suits were unsuccessful. In fact, the competitors ended up having to license the technology from ABSea Company under royalty agreements totaling $30 million.

You can locate qualified accounting and legal firms by networking with your board members, technical advisors, CEO's of other start-ups, and Angel investment groups.

THE SEA: LARGE MARKET POTENTIAL

Now that you have a strong Captain CEO and experienced crew on board, it's time to choose your territory. All of your boat's activities take place on the sea of the market place. You will claim a valuable section of that sea as your own. Once you've identified and captured your territory, you will mine its riches. While it is possible, in an extremely large market, for the company to succeed with an average product or with a less than stellar management team, this is clearly not the most desirable situation.

For many VC's, market potential is by far the most important element of the voyage. If the treasures are small, why sail out into a potentially turbulent sea full of obstacles and risk losing the investment?

Start out by figuring out the best place to stake your claim. Use "market research" to define the market potential in terms of:

⚓ **Qualification of Size**

Overall market size and size of market segment addressed by your company's product

⚓ **Stage**

Market Segment's stage of the market lifecycle

⚓ **Trend**

Direction market is headed

⚓ **Share**

Amount of the qualified market you need to make your financial forecast

Since this is such an important part of your map, let's take a closer look at each of the factors that make up **Market Potential.**

Qualification of Size of Market

Who are the customers who will buy your cargo? Where are they located in the sea of the market? Your first market research endeavor should be to determine the size, in terms of sales revenues, of the total market addressed by your company's product, over the next 3 to 5 years. This gives VC's a sense of the breadth of the market and how much potential there is for future expansion into multiple market segments. Also, as products are being developed and time goes on, the market dynamics, in terms of product requirements, may change and there must be room to maneuver.

How large does the total potential market have to be? An ideal market is one with $500 million or more in gross revenues today and $ 1 billion or more in your window of the next 3 to 5 years. With this market size, if you can gain a 5% market share in 5 years, your revenues would be on the order of $50 million, which makes this a reasonable venture for VC's to consider. Of course this varies with the stage the market is in and projected growth rate, as well as with how much of the market your product can capture.

The next step to market qualification is crucial and one that sinks many start-up boats. Although you may have identified a large market, you must now segment that market into the piece(s) that your products directly address.

From The Old Salt's Journal

Why is identifying the size of the market for your initial products so important? Let's take an example case study:

> *ABSea Company is a start-up in the field of wooden oars. They have developed a new, patented design of a product that will improve performance at a lower cost. This is very valuable cargo. They have an excellent crew led by Captain CEO and a viable treasure map (business plan), but have not reached VC Funding Island. The obstacle is they are facing is the size of the qualified market.*

> *Although the total market is projected to grow from $30 million this year to $600 million in 5 years, the market segment ABSea Company addresses is only $10 million this year and projected to be $120 million in 5 years. They would have to capture 42% of the market to build a $50 million company in a very competitive market. Sizing the market risk factors and the amount of the investment needed, ($20 million), the VC's have not invested and the boat has not left the dock.*

Market Stages

The lifecycle of a market consists of four stages:

⚓ **Embryonic**

New products that address a quantifiable market need are identified. Initial products are prepared for market entry. Companies make a large investment in R&D.

⚓ **Growth**

Once the market needs and product acceptance are established, products begin to be produced and distributed in volume to meet the growing market demands. Many companies compete for market share.

⚓ **Mature**

Rate of market growth slows and only the best companies survive.

⚓ **Aging**

Size of market flattens out and begins to decline. Companies begin harvesting the market to maximize their profits and begin exiting the market.

There are also four potential Positions of a company in a market:

⚓ **Weak/Tenable**

Small and losing market share, unprofitable, non-competitive products

⚓ **Favorable**

Building customer base and strategic alliances, good revenue growth and introducing new, competitive products

⚓ **Strong**

At least 15% market share, in a shared leadership position with at least one other significant company

⚓ **Dominant**

At least 30% market share, other companies follow your actions. There can only be one dominant company

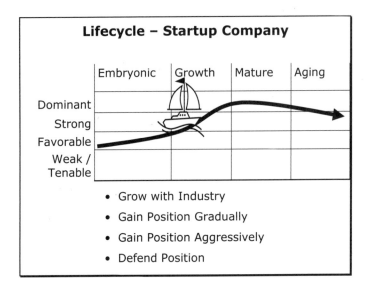

The line across the chart shows the typical life cycle of a start-up company. The cycle begins with market entry and the company growing with the market. Then the rate of success will be determined by whether the company gains market share gradually or aggressively, and by how well it's able to defend its position.

The ideal position for a start-up is to begin in a favorable or strong position of a market that is just beginning to enter the growth stage.

Market Trend

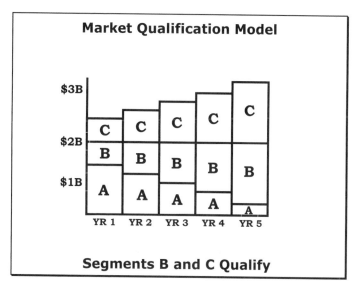

Unfortunately, as we have learned from the past few years, the direction of the marketplace is not always up. Even in a growth cycle, not all segments of a market will have positive growth. Some segments may grow rapidly while others show little or no growth and still others may decline. You need to be sure your products address the growth segments.

Market Qualification Model

Segments B and C Qualify

For example, this chart shows a total market at $2.5 billion growing to $3 billion over 5 years. The market is made up of 3 major segments **A**, **B**, and **C**. Segment **A** is declining and segment **B** is taking over its position. Segment **C** is growing with the overall market.

Which segment would you like to have your company address? The company with products in segment **C** is clearly more attractive than companies addressing segments **A** or **B**.

Why not **B**? Companies in segment **B** gain market share by taking it away from segment **A**. It is a much harder task to take market share away from companies that are entrenched in a market than to compete for a share of the added growth in a market.

Market Share

There are two factors you need to consider when determining the amount of market share you will need to project, to qualify as a potential VC investment.

First, there is the percent of the qualified market segment needed to make your financial projections. VC's are looking for companies that meet projected revenues with a 5% to 10% market share. The higher the percentage of market needed, the higher the risk.

The second factor: What is the company's potential to gain enough market share to become a significant player in the market?   If the company has the potential to capture 20% to 30% or more, then the company is deemed to have significant up-side potential and becomes an attractive, potential investment.

From The Old Salt's Journal

The Plastic Anchor Company (PAC) had a good, new product idea. The problem was that the market segment the product addressed was only $160 million. Although the market was projected to be entering a growth cycle, in order to meet their third year revenue projection of $60 million, the company would either; a) have to gain a dominant market share position of nearly 40% if the market did not grow or b) have to gain a 10% market share if the market grew by an incredible 1,000% to $600 million.

In either case, many VC's and private investors concluded the market risk was too high and did not invest. The company finally did secure seed funding from private investors and two small VC firms. Although the product was good, the market sector was very competitive and the market grew by only 4%. The result was that PAC had very low revenues and could not attract additional funding. The company went into bankruptcy and the investors lost all of their investment.

**Obstacle #4
Size of Qualified Market**

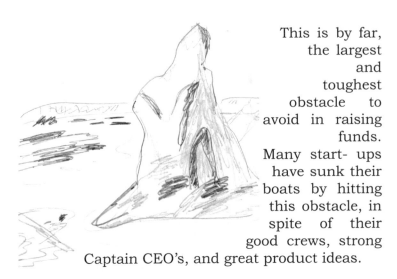

This is by far, the largest and toughest obstacle to avoid in raising funds. Many start- ups have sunk their boats by hitting this obstacle, in spite of their good crews, strong Captain CEO's, and great product ideas.

Over 90% of the potential funding opportunities are rejected due to the lack of significant market potential. This does not mean you cannot have a successful small company. It does mean that the funding will have to come from sources other than VC's.

TACK & JIBE

The challenge is to find a way to increase the size of the qualified market segments. One option may be to re-define your product as a market entry version with the objective of reducing the all-important "time to market."   Then identify follow-on versions, with additional features and functions that broaden the scope of the market, and add them to the product "family."

Another possibility is to enrich the initial product design with functionality that addresses more of the needs of a larger market.

A third possibility is to develop multiple products, related to the initial core product, which address additional market segments. Whatever product strategy you develop, the qualified market must be large enough to avoid sinking the boat.

**For Smooth Sailing
Past Obstacle #4**

**Large Qualified Market,
Early Growth Stage, Upward
Trend**

The ideal situation VC's are looking for, to qualify for investment is:

**A company that has a
business model
map to profitability
within 18 months,**

**generates at least $50 million
in revenues in 3 to 5 years
with a market share of
5% to 10%,**

**and is in an early stage
growth market with
significant upside potential.**

CARGO: SUPERIOR PRODUCT

Most entrepreneurs believe that if they have a great product idea, the VC's will line up to invest. Nothing could be farther from the truth. The fact is, VC's **expect** you to have a dynamite product idea.

They will determine the potential value of your product by getting the answers to these questions:

⚓ What exactly is the product and what are its features and benefits?

⚓ What is the product's differentiation?

⚓ What are the product's competitive advantages?

⚓ Where is the product in terms of technology life cycle?

⚓ What is the status of product development?

- ⚓ Who is the customer?

- ⚓ What market needs does the product meet?

- ⚓ What factors will a customer consider in selecting the product?

- ⚓ Who is the competition?

- ⚓ How does the product compare to the competitors' product?

- ⚓ What are the barriers to market entry?

- ⚓ Is there any early market acceptance?

- ⚓ What are the barriers to market acceptance?

- ⚓ Have you formed any strategic alliances?

- ⚓ How will the product be marketed?

You will need to be prepared to answer each of these questions, in detail. How prepared you are and the substance of each answer, will be vital to your journey. Let's explore each question and see how each relates to the funding decision.

What exactly is the product and what are its features and benefits?

You have to know your cargo and be able to articulate its merits.

From The Old Salt's Journal

During my career at IBM, I had exposure to many of the future management stars as they worked their way up the ladder. In one meeting, a regional manager was presenting a new product idea for the aerospace industry to the President of the Division.

In those ancient times, presentations were made using large, paper flip charts. Each page was done with multicolor markers and listed the major points in large lettering. Just as the regional manager was about to start his presentation, the president asked, "Ralph, how many charts do you have?" Ralph replied, 46.

The president then said, "Ralph, if it takes 46 charts to describe a product, either the product is too complex or you don't understand it yourself. Get out of here and come back when you can describe it in one chart."

Ralph came back two weeks later, with one chart and a better understanding of the product. By the way, Ralph went on to become President of IBM

To help communicate your product idea to people of varying background and interest, **you need to be able to explain what your product is and does in 25 words or less**. Here is an example of a product description, from the telecommunications industry:

Product Description:
A very high-speed modem for home and office use that supports high bandwidth applications on the Internet, such as full motion video.

This brief description tells what the product is, what market it addresses, and some of its features and benefits.

Feature	Benefit
Up to 50 mbps data rates	More applications can be supported such as music and video down loads
Highly integrated design	Low manufacturing cost
Meets industry standards	Easy to install and operate

Many entrepreneurs get caught up in the wiz bang features of a product. A potential investor may respond, "so what?"   Product features have little meaning unless they produce benefits for the customer. **The market buys benefits that meet customer needs, not technical features.**

Prepare to talk to investors about your cargo. Create a brief product description of 25 words or less and be able to relate the product's features to resulting benefits to the customer.

What is the product's differentiation?

What makes your cargo special?   This is a major factor that VC's will hone in on. As one very high profile VC once asked, "What's the hook?" He was asking, "what makes this product unique and sets it high above the competition?"

You will need a differentiator to avoid being lumped together with other companies having a "me to" product. Although lower cost is important, it is not enough of a differentiator by itself to excite the investment community. Combine lower cost with greater performance and added functionality and you attract VC interest.

For example, your product could:

- ⚓ Provide significant performance improvement without equipment changes or large capital expenditures

- ⚓ Fill a void in systems architecture

- ⚓ Provide a means for productivity improvements

- ⚓ Result in large cost savings without deterioration of services

- ⚓ Open access to additional applications and markets

Obstacle #5
Not Enough Product Differentiation

TACK & JIBE

The key here is market research.   You must understand the needs of the customer, the competition, and the market trends.   Use this information to define the market requirements. Define the product specification to meet and exceed these requirements.   Some actions that could strengthen your differentiation factor are:

- ⚓ Add more product performance

- ⚓ Introduce new functionality

- ⚓ Reduce manufacturing cost while adding functionality and/or performance

- ⚓ Take advantage of new technology and patent protection for extra 'value added'

- ⚓ Broaden the scope of applications

- ⚓ Improve "ease of use" and/or "ease of installation"

- ⚓ Create or increase compatibility with current products

Your product needs to have enough differentiation to "hook" the VC.

**For Smooth Sailing
Past Obstacle #5**

**Develop Products with
"Added Value"
Differentiation that
Addresses Customer Needs
and Market Trends**

Where is the product in terms of technology life cycle?

As one CEO, who has founded several successful startups likes to say, "The challenge and reward is making successful business out of a technology." There are two phases of a technology's life cycle that we are interested in:

Revolution
⚓ Has a dramatic impact on the ways things are done

⚓ Examples:
> Light Bulb
> TV
> Mainframe Computer
> Remote Data
>> Communications
>> Network

Evolution
⚓ Follow-on improvements that build on the implementations of a technology over time

⚓ Examples:
> Halogen Light Bulbs
> HDTV
> Lap Top PC's
> The Internet

VC's prefer evolutionary technology and rarely fund companies based on revolutionary technology.

Why? The life cycle from Revolution, (technology discovery), to Evolution (practical application and acceptance) is normally too long. The first TV prototype was demonstrated on September 9, 1927. It was not till the late 1940's, that commercial products began to be accepted in volume.

Remember, the VC fund has a life of 5 to 7 years and the typical technology life cycle, from Revolution to Evolution, is on the order of 12 years.   Think Evolutionary products not Revolutionary technology.

What is the status of product development?

Is your cargo ready to load onto the boat? There are five stages from developing a product concept to shipping it to the first customer.

PLANNING	Defining the product specifications.
PROOF OF CONCEPT	Product modeling and performance simulation. Build basic prototype.
ALPHA	Working prototype for testing and demonstration.
BETA	Controlled release of field evaluation units to limited number of customer sites.
MARKET ENTRY	First shipments of product to market.

Naturally, the closer you are to having a finished product, the more investor interest you will command. As you execute your product development plan, it becomes easier to evaluate the market potential and also reduces the size and risk of investment. Your progress also demonstrates your ability to meet project milestones and control spending. Both are strong positive attributes to VC's.

Another potentially strong plus with VC's is offshore product development. If your product is of the type that a significant amount of the development work can be done offshore, with minimum risk, then your development cost will be lower and your funding coins will go farther. This could result in fewer future rounds of raising coins and less ownership dilution.

A trap some start-ups fall into is trying to develop the "perfect product." There comes a time in the product development cycle when **"good enough is good enough."** That's when it's time to freeze the design and get the product into the market.

From The Old Salt's Journal
I have seen cases where the "fine tuning" of the product took an additional six months or more, with little added value, and cost companies up to a third of the market.

It is as challenging to quickly and efficiently commercialize a product, as it is to develop it.

Who is the customer?

Who wants your cargo?   The customer can be defined at four levels. Each level narrows the market until the person who will make the buying decision is identified:

⚓ **Industry/Industries addressed**
First pass at defining customer market segment.

⚓ **Type and size of companies**
List of the top 6 prospect companies.

⚓ **Organization/Department**
What part of the company has a need for your product?

⚓ **Title of "decision maker"**
Person who will take responsibility for deciding to buy your product.

Many start-ups can go to the level of naming potential customer companies but have had little or no actual customer contact. The more positive customer feedback you have, the more credibility you will gain with VC's. Some VC's now require a start-up to have customers lined-up and committed to buy the product or even to have generated revenues of at least $1 million.

What needs does the product meet?

Why do the customers want your cargo? In order to convince someone to buy your product, it must meet one or more business or personal needs. Whatever the needs, it is best if they are definable and quantifiable. Some examples:

- ⚓ Cost savings

- ⚓ Time savings

- ⚓ Increased reliability

- ⚓ Improved performance

- ⚓ Better ease of use

- ⚓ Reduced error rates

- ⚓ Reduced stress, accidents

- ⚓ Enhanced appearance, health

You must be able to show how your product can meet the customer's needs in a way that justifies the buying decision.

What factors will the customer consider in selecting the product?

This brings us to an area that can have a big influence on the VC's decision to invest. The customer decision maker will use several key factors to assess the value proposition of your product and to compare it to the competition. Identifying those key factors can be very useful in gaining customers. Unfortunately, many start-ups neglect this area. They either fail to identify or fail to leverage their knowledge of the customer's decision factors.

Some examples of decision factors:

⚓ Performance

⚓ Availability

⚓ Price

⚓ Vendor viability

⚓ Service and support

By talking to decision makers and listening to their product requirements, you can gain valuable insight into your customer's decision-making process.

Another important point is that not all factors are of equal value in the buying decision. For example, some customers are willing to pay a higher price premium of 10% to 15% to do business with a vendor company where they have good relationships and experiences, versus an unknown start-up. Other customers will not consider vendors with weak service or weak support.

You should develop a list of the top 5 to 10 factors that most of your potential customers will use in comparing product offerings and making the buy decision.

Who is the competition?

Are there Pirates after your cargo?

The worst possible answer:

"No. There is no competition."

This is a strong, negative signal that either there is not enough of a market to attract competitors, or that you have not done a good job in researching the market and the competition. You should be able to list your top 5 competitors along with their strengths and weaknesses. You will lose credibility if the VC's technical staff knows more about the competition than you do. Your competitive position will be a factor in setting the company's valuation.

How does your product compare to the competitors' products?

You will be expected to show a side-by-side comparison of your product's functions and features to the competition's product. The traditional method is to use a matrix or table of comparisons.

In this example, we are showing how our product stacks up versus the competition.

	Our Widget	Comp A	Comp B	Comp C
Price	Lo	Hi	Hi	Lo
Integrate ability	Hi	Hi	Lo	Hi
Power Consumption	Lo	Lo	Hi	Lo
Service ability	Hi	Lo	Hi	Hi
Reliability	Hi	Hi	Lo	Lo
Performance	Hi	Hi	Hi	Lo

VC's are very used to this approach, so they can relate to this way of presenting information about competitive position. On the other hand, VC's sit through many meetings looking for fresh thinking and new approaches. This is one area where you can gain some advantage over the competition for funding.

One way to take the competitive analysis a step further is to add another matrix. First, we can show our relative strength versus competitors, on a feature-by-feature basis:

S = we are stronger

E = we are equal

W = we are weaker

	Comp A	Comp B	Comp C
Price	S	S	W
Integrate ability	E	S	S
Power Consumption	W	S	E
Service ability	S	W	E
Reliability	S	E	E
Performance	E	E	S

Second, we can highlight those features that customers have told us are the most important to them. This is an effective way to show that we have a superior set of features that best fits customer needs. The stronger you make a case for being superior to the competition, the more likely to gain VC interest.

**Obstacle #6
Weak Competitive Position**

TACK & JIBE

The key to matching up favorably against competition is to stress your product's differentiation strengths; particularly those features and functions that are on the customer selection criteria list. That is, focus on those features and functions that are most important to a particular customer.

The sales tactics for each customer should include getting the customer to place more value on your product's differentiation and/or to place less value on the competition's product functions and features. You may not be able to match all of the competition's strong points, but you can reduce their influence on the customer's buying decision.

**For Smooth Sailing
Past Obstacle #6**

**Use presentation methods
and models that show your
product in the best
competitive light**

What are the barriers to market entry?

Keep the pirates out of your territory. The harder it is for others to enter your market segment and compete directly against your product, the higher your chances to succeed, and the more attractive is the investment opportunity. Early market entry is critical for a new company in establishing a customer base that, once committed, is hard to dislodge. The question VC's will ask is "what will prevent other companies that have more money and more people, from doing the same type of product?" Your answer will weigh heavily on their investment decision.

Some examples of viable market entry barriers are:

- ⚓ Requires technical skills that are hard to find and take a long time to learn.

- ⚓ Defines a "de-facto" standard or industry standard that competition must follow.

- ⚓ Have intellectual property (PATENTS) that will limit the competitors' ability to use the same processes and technologies in product development.

- ⚓ Product design and development cycle is so complex that it will take competitors a significant amount of time to enter the market.

Obstacle #7
Low Barriers to Market Entry

TACK & JIBE

The investors will want some form of market entry barrier to help protect their investment. That is, there should be something that will prevent your competition from quickly or easily entering your market. The fact that you are able to produce a product at lower cost may not be enough of a barrier, as others will eventually get their cost down. Do not overlook the possibility of patenting your product.

From The Old Salt's Journal

I know one start-up company that was "too busy" to file for patents. While they were frantically working on their day-to-day priorities, one of their alliance companies filed the patents on their technology and gained a significant market position.

Never get so busy that you don't protect your technology.

Enter the market ASAP, even if it's with a basic, limited features product. Having an early market position gives you market acceptance and establishes you in a market leadership role. Once customers design-in your product, it may be time consuming and expensive for them to change when competitors enter the market.

Another consideration is, as an early market entrant, you may be able to lock up key commitments from suppliers and distribution channels that will make market entry more difficult for the competition.

**For Smooth Sailing
Past Obstacle #7**

Protect your position and technology. Create exclusive relationships and Patent. Patent. Patent.

Is there any early market acceptance?

Any signal that there is customer interest in your product is a positive indicator to potential investors. The stronger the early market acceptance, the easier it is to gauge market demand.

There are a number of ways to demonstrate early product acceptance:

Establish test sites with major potential customers

⚓ Provides valuable feedback on product performance, usability, and suggestions for enhancements and improvements.

⚓ Leads to early sales.

Secure Letters of Intent

⚓ Shows commitment to purchase product once it becomes available.

<u>Gain Recognition from industry trade</u>
<u>associations and standards bodies</u>

⚓ Makes it much easier
to market the product.
Many large customers
will not buy products
that are based on
proprietary technology
and/or do not meet
industry standards.

**Obstacle #8
No Early Market Acceptance**

TACK & JIBE

If your product is not at the stage where you can do any of the above, the next best thing is to solicit comments and testimonials from people within the industry who are well recognized and respected. Chief Technical Officers of major companies, college professors who are experts in this area, industry consultants, and writers for industry publications are all excellent sources.

**For Smooth Sailing
Past Obstacle #8**

**Signal support of your
product to investors by
securing statements from
customers or credible allies**

What are the barriers to market acceptance?

It's important to know your weaknesses, as well as your strengths, and to be able to articulate them.

There can be several barriers to market acceptance. Some of the most common are:

- ⚓ Customers must make major changes to their current applications

- ⚓ High capital expenditures are required

- ⚓ Unproven technology

- ⚓ Proprietary non-standard products

- ⚓ Specialized skills are needed to install and support

- ⚓ Multi-vendor involvement is necessary

- ⚓ Must replace current suppliers product

Obstacle #9
Many Barriers to Market Acceptance

TACK & JIBE

Barriers are not complete "sinkers" but they sure can toss your ship around and slow you down. They can cause real damage if not recognized and accounted for. Barriers make the selling job much tougher; so the more of them that you can remove the smoother the ride. It is important to recognize a barrier and if you cannot remove it, you need to have a strategy to neutralize it.

**For Smooth Sailing
Past Obstacle #9**

**Modify product to remove
or neutralize barriers and
'sell-around' them.**

Have you formed any Strategic Alliances?

In today's market, it is very difficult to go it alone. One of the best actions you can take is

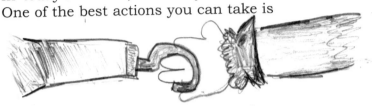

to form one or more strategic alliances with major companies in your industry.

There can be many positive benefits to your company:

⚓ Added sales channels

⚓ Instant credibility

⚓ Access to expertise

⚓ Source of funding

⚓ Potential future merger

⚓ Access to complementary technology

⚓ Save time and money

VC's place heavy emphasis on having good strategic alliances. Alliances can take many shapes from loose marketing relationships to major joint development agreements.

**Obstacle #10
Too Few Strategic Alliances**

TACK & JIBE

Make high quality alliances. The best alliances have both companies investing people and effort. You must, however, be very careful to protect the intellectual property assets of your company and to ensure that the relationship yields results that benefit both companies. Sometimes start-ups are so anxious to work with a large company that they enter into an agreement that causes them to lose control over their technology and eventually put the company at risk.

**For Smooth Sailing
Past Obstacle #10**

Create high quality and mutually beneficial relationships with strategic companies.

How will the product be marketed?

How are you going to move that cargo? So far, you have shown that you have a product with large market potential and enough differentiation to beat the competition. Too often, start-ups think this is enough; the VC's will invest and the customers will line up to buy. This is an attitude that can sink your boat. You need to form a sales and marketing strategy that shows how you are going to enter the market, quickly capture market share, and grow sales revenues.

The marketing plan should drive on the product strengths and value-added differentiation to capture the mindset of customers. Some effective marketing activities are:

- ⚓ Advertising campaigns

- ⚓ Industry trade shows and conferences

- ⚓ Articles in industry publications

- ⚓ Professional societies' meetings

- ⚓ Sales and marketing alliances

- ⚓ Promoting joint development agreements

- ⚓ Key account focus programs

The sales plan must demonstrate the ability to ramp up sales quickly and should address what sales channels will be used:

⚓ Direct sales force

⚓ Distributors

⚓ Value Added Resellers (VARS)

⚓ In house sales (telemarketing, web site)

⚓ License to third parties

In many cases, the old 80/20 Rule will apply. That is, 80 percent of the sales will come from 20 percent of the customers. If this applies to your product, your sales and marketing strategy must show how you are focusing your efforts and resources on the key customers.

One of the best ways to impress VC's is to have a sales and marketing strategy that shows how you are going to leverage your strategic alliances into sales. Having commitments for sales from one or more large customers is one of the most significant indicators that you have a viable and marketable product and gives you far more credibility than just showing a large potential market.

Obstacle #11
Weak Marketing and Sales Strategy

TACK & JIBE

As the chart shows, once you understand how your product fills the needs of customers and the weaknesses of competitors, you can develop marketing and sales programs that focus on this area. If you need help, you may want to add someone with a strong skill set in this area to your crew or to bring extra hands on deck in the form of a qualified consultant.

> **For Smooth Sailing
> Past Obstacle #11**
>
> **Develop Strong Marketing
> and Sales Plans that Target
> Key Customers.**

WEATHER: THE FINANCIALS

Good forecasting can help you avoid sailing into major storms. A big issue with investors will be the ability of the company to raise enough money to get to a position of positive cash flow. To assess the probability of success, VC's will analyze a number of financial factors. Depending on the particular VC, the complexity of the financial analysis can vary greatly. We will not over burden you with financial models and statistical analysis techniques, but will introduce you to the critical financial factors that most VC's require.

**If you only remember one
critical financial
factor, remember that**

CASH IS KING.

The Burn Rate

Basically, the burn rate is how much money the start-up is spending each month. The VC's will look at the burn rate in terms of:

⚓ How long will the cash on hand last?

⚓ Is it enough to make it through till the company cash flow turns positive?

That is:

**Cash Flow = Money In (revenues & prior funding)
– Money Out (all cash spent)**

An "end of cash" analysis should be prepared each month to provide a clear picture of how much longer the company can exist with the cash on hand.

Many start-ups make the mistake of waiting until they have less than six months of cash left before they try to raise more funding. Waiting and running low on cash can sink your boat.

**Obstacle #12
Burn Rate Increasing Over a Period of
3 Years**

TACK & JIBE

VC's will not usually invest in a company that plans to increase the burn rate for 3 or more years. They may be concerned that the company will run out of cash. Every effort should be made to conserve cash and keep the burn rate down. Many start-ups spend cash in certain areas before it is really necessary and put strain on the cash flow.

Examples include ramping up the manufacturing operations before sales come in, or establishing and staffing multiple sales offices before the product is ready for release. The questions to ask are:

⚓ Does this expenditure relate directly to meeting a critical milestone?

⚓ If not, can it be eliminated, reduced, or rescheduled to a time when more cash is available?

**For Smooth Sailing
Past Obstacle #12**

**Conserve Cash. Spend only
on necessary and timely
business activities.**

Path to Profitability

Investors want to know when the company will break even and consistently earn profits. Once the company turns profitable, it can fund its own operations and will no longer be in need of additional funding. In today's market, VC's like to see at least 3 months in a row of positive cash flow starting within 18 months of funding.

While getting to break even in a short amount of time is very important, VC's are slowly once again becoming more comfortable with assuming more risk in projects that will take more time to break even. They are willing to invest for the longer term, as long as there is a promise of higher returns on their investment.

**Obstacle #13
Long Path to Profitability**

TACK & JIBE

The "Path to Profitability" ties into managing the burn rate to conserve cash and focus early marketing and sales efforts on generating revenues. One option to shorten the path may be to develop a basic product that has fundamental functions and features. Use this product for early release to enter the market, establish a beachhead, and begin generating revenues. Then follow-up with product releases that have a fuller set of features.

**For Smooth Sailing
Past Obstacle #13**

**Shorten Path to Profitability
by tightly managing cash
flow; focusing on early
revenue generation and
early market entry.**

Forecasting the Weather:
Financial Projections

To forecast your cash flow, burn rate, and Path to Profitability you will need to develop a set of financial projections. We suggest you do 3 years worth of projections in detail: by month for the first year and quarterly for the next two years. Take into account all sources of cash and all expenses. Sources of cash include investor funds and sales revenues. Expenses include: people, equipment, facilities, sales and marketing programs, and product production ramp up.

You will need three forms of projections. Your accountant or financial person can produce the forms once the detailed data is made available.

⚓ **Balance Sheet**	Snapshot of the company's financial position at a point in time
⚓ **Net Income Statement**	Key report. Shows revenues, margins, expenses, profitability
⚓ **Cash Flow Analysis**	Shows cash position, burn rate, how long it will last

For each year of projections, list any assumptions and do 3 versions:

Worst Case Scenario:

Torrential Downpours, Tornados, Hurricanes, etc. Forcing Your Boat to Proceed Very Slowly:
Obtain 50% to 70% of revenues

Expected Case Scenario:

A few Obstacles but Weathering the Storm:
100% of revenues

Best Case Scenario:

Sunny Skies and Smooth Sailing all the Way:
125% to 150% of revenues

The VC's will key on the Worst Case Scenario. They will look at your assumptions and do some of their own analysis. Since it can be difficult to forecast financials for a start-up, doing 3 scenarios gives the VC's a broader scope to work with and shows you have done a good job of financial planning. This also helps you to prepare you for the time when you will be in front of the VC and asked questions like:

- ⚓ What market share is being projected?

- ⚓ What are the main sources of revenues and what are the probabilities of getting them?

- ⚓ What are the main factors affecting gross margins?

- ⚓ What is the growth rate and what assumptions did you use?

- ⚓ How much cash will be required and in what time period?

- ⚓ How long and how much cash to design and develop the prototype product?

- ⚓ How long and how much cash to design, test, and evaluate the manufacturing process?

- ⚓ How long and how much cash to get the required regulatory approvals?

How well the crew answers these questions helps to convince the VC's that they fully understand the financials, will control spending, and will strictly manage the cash flow.

Scalability

Are you planning to make your boat bigger in the future? Do you foresee adding more boats to create your own fleet? When VC's refer to "scalability" they are referring to a business that can grow rapidly. Rapid growth is the way a company produces worthwhile returns for investors. In addressing scalability, the associated cost to support rapid growth must also be considered. High cost is the downside risk that has caused many start-up boats to sink. For example, many Internet companies were considered to be highly scalable, but the huge cost of marketing caused them to have high burn rates that ate up their cash and they ended up going bankrupt.

Not all VC's have the same guidelines when it comes to scalability. A reasonable set of guidelines is:

With investment up to $1 million	⚓ Can you show proof of product concept?
With investment up to $5 million	⚓ Can you build product prototype and secure customer test sites?
With investment up to $10 million	⚓ Can you begin producing and shipping market entry product?

Obstacle #14   Poor Scalability

TACK & JIBE

The degree of scalability goes hand in hand with the market opportunity factors. That is why it so important to have products that address large markets and can be ramped up quickly with reasonable cost. You may need to re-visit the addressable market issue, and fine tune your product value-added differentiators to meet the scalability guidelines.

**For Smooth Sailing
Past Obstacle #14**

Conserve cash so business can grow rapidly without draining funds. Adjust market placement and/or product differentiation to increase growth rate.

Exit Strategy

There comes the time, when the VC's will want to cash in on their investment. This is when they will reap the benefits of having invested in you and in your boat.   Options are to sell the company, to merge with a public company, or to do an initial public offering (IPO).

Initial Public Offering (IPO)

When there is a high demand for private equity, as there was during the wave of strong momentum for "dot com" companies in1998 through 1999, it was relatively easy to do an IPO. After the bubble burst, the window of opportunity closed and in the second half of 2000 and for a long time thereafter, there were very few IPO's. VC's expect 10% to 15% of their companies will do an IPO. Nevertheless, they will demand the right to take every company public.

Sell/Merge

Most companies will exit by either selling or merging. The question is, to whom and when?

⚓ Sell/Merge Candidates

o   Joint venture partners

o   Alliances

o   Competitors

o   Companies that need to fill a product gap

⚓ When to Sell

o   Premiums usually higher early in product life cycle

o   Higher valuations when company revenues are trending up

o   Buyers looking for strategic fit

It is a good idea to have an exit plan even if it is only a list of potential sell/merge candidates. Too often, start-ups just assume they will do an IPO.

Part 3
Drawing the Map to
VC Funding Island

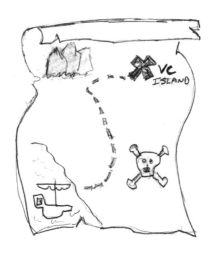

At The Ship Yard

Up to this point, we have been working to prepare your boat and cargo, and planning your route to avoid obstacles in the four main areas of the business model:

- ⚓ People

- ⚓ Market Opportunity

- ⚓ Product Offering

- ⚓ Financials

Before setting sail and going out to look for funds, we must have a clear idea of how much trading power we'll have when we get there.   We need to take a good look at our boat and figure out how much it's worth, plus how much of it we want to trade to investors and at what price.

Sizing Up the Boat
"How to Value a Company"

How Much Is Your Boat Worth to Investors? The last important topic that must be addressed before we can put it all together is the topic of company valuation. This is one of the first items that VC's raise and if the valuation is not in line with their investment criteria, then there is no need to waste your time or theirs, end of conversation.

Since the process of coming up with a valuation includes both tangible and intangible factors, it can prove to be a very emotional and difficult issue for the founders of the company. Many high potential deals get killed because founders place such a high value on their efforts that there is little chance for the VC's to make a reasonable return on their investment. To better understand what it takes to produce a "win – win" scenario, let's look at the pieces that need to fit together to attract and close funding.

Valuation Part 1 of 3
How Much Funding To Raise

First you must decide how much money to raise. This is a very important decision. Remember, you are giving up a part of the ownership in exchange for the money. The more money raised, the less you own and the more the investors own. The guideline is to raise enough money to meet an initial set of milestones that show meaningful progress for the company. It is crucial that you raise enough money to reach reasonable milestones. If there is not enough money, or if the milestones are too aggressive, you will end up at the mercy of the VC's.

Smooth Sailing Company Example

As an example, let's assume the Smooth Sailing Company (SSC) determines it needs to raise $1 million in order to build and launch its boat.

Once we have an amount of money needed in mind, we take a look at how it will affect the funding structure. There are two forms of valuation:

- ⚓ **Pre**-money value
- ⚓ **Post**-money value

Pre-Money

"Pre-money" value is the value of your company (or SSC's boat) <u>before</u> the VC's make an investment. For SSC, let's assume that we have developed a product (prepared our cargo) and are positioned to enter the marketplace via several initial orders from customers who have the potential to buy in high volumes. We have assessed our current position and have come to a pre-money valuation for our boat of $3million.

This is very important to the VC's as it determines how much ownership they will get for their investment. The equity given equals the amount of the VC investment divided by the sum of the pre-money value and the VC investment.

$$\text{Equity to VC's (\% Ownership)} = \frac{\text{VC's Investment}}{\text{Pre-money value} + \text{VC's Investment}}$$

$$\text{Equity to VC's} = \frac{\$1 \text{ million}}{\$3 \text{ million} + \$1 \text{ million}} = \frac{\$1 \text{ million}}{\$4 \text{ million}}$$

$$\text{Equity to VC's} = 25\%$$

When VC's ask for your valuation, it's the pre-money number they want to know.

Post-Money

"Post-money" value is the value of the company <u>after</u> the VC investment. That is, pre-money value plus VC's investment. In the case of SSC's boat, $3 million + $1 million = $4 million post value. VC's use post-money value to estimate how much money your company (or SSC's boat) must generate when it goes public or is sold, for the investment to be successful.

Company Valuation Methods

There are several methods VC's can use in determining the future value of the company:

⚓ **Comparison to similar type companies in the same industry**
   Changing market conditions could make these types of comparisons unrealistic.

⚓ **Using a multiple factor times projected yearly revenues or times projected earnings**
   VC's may use a higher or lower multiple based on current market conditions.

⚓ **Discounted Cash Flow (DCF) or Net Present Value Method**
   The value of the company is based on the amount of cash flow generated over several years. To many VC's, this is the best way to determine valuation.

Valuation is determined by the combination of factors:

- ⚓ How solid is the business model?

- ⚓ Do the comparables or the DCF method project a reasonable and workable valuation?

- ⚓ What is the going rate?   That is, what is the market willing to pay?

- ⚓ Does the amount of the investment fall into the range of this VC's investment pattern?

- ⚓ In the case of SSC's Boat, if the VC usually invests from $1 million to $2 million for 20% to 35% of a Boat on an expedition of this type (in this industry segment), then there is a fit.

Dilution and Future Fund Raising

Another factor that affects valuation is the likelihood of needing to raise more funds with one or more future rounds of fund raising. With each round, the crew ends ups with a smaller percentage of ownership. That is, their equity position is diluted. The amount of dilution will depend on how quickly the value of the company is growing, staying the same, or decreasing. If additional rounds are in fact required, a new VC will often lead them. Remember to keep focused. No one likes to see their equity position diluted, but less equity is a far better position than going down with the ship due to lack of funds.

Now let's look at the final two pieces of the funding equation, the liquidity event and the hurdle rate.

Valuation Part 2 of 3
Liquidity Event

The liquidity event is how the VC's make their money. Either the company has an Initial Public Offering (IPO) or the company is sold. The timing of the liquidity event is usually within 3 to 5 years of funding but could be as short as 2 years or as long as 7 years.

Valuation Part 3 of 3
Hurdle Rate

The last piece of information needed is for the VC's to determine how much money they can expect to earn on their investment. The yearly compound percentage rate of return on their investment is called the hurdle rate. This is the minimum (hurdle) percentage of earnings that they are willing to accept for the amount of time their money is tied up and for the amount of risk in the investment. Some guidelines:

Investment Stage	Hurdle Rate %
Seed – Start Up	60+
First – Early Stage	40 to 60
Second – Profitable Company	30 to 40
Third - Profitable Company	20 to 30
Bridge to Liquidity Event	20

As the table shows, the higher the perceived risk, the higher the rate-of-return needed to do the investment. VC's justify high hurdle rates in the fact that start-ups have no public market and the rate must take into account that there may be future equity dilution in later funding rounds.

Smooth Sailing Company Example

In our example, SSC's boat's pre-money valuation is $3 million, and the investment target is to raise $1million for which SSC is willing to give up 25% ownership resulting in a post-money value of $4 million. If the boat will be sold in 5 years and the hurdle rate is 50%, how much must the boat be sold for, in order to be a do-able investment for the VCs?

Hurdle Rate % (5 years)	Sale Price
35	18 million
50	30 million
100	128 million

For their $1 million investment, after 5 years and at a 50% hurdle rate, the VCs would get $7.5 million (25% of $30 million). If SSC were a third stage investment, the sale price would only need to be $18 million, but if it were a seed stage start-up, the sales price would jump to $128 million. You can now see why VC's invest in high growth companies.

The general guideline is that VC's expect to earn in excess of 5 times their investment over 5 years.   One of the VC's who we work with often likes to say, "The longer the voyage, the longer our money is at risk and the higher the expected treasure."

Gold Nuggets:

⚓ VCs have most of the leverage when it comes to valuations. They have many opportunities to invest while you may have limited money-raising options.

⚓ Try to position the strengths of the business model before addressing valuation. Bringing it up too soon could send a negative message to the VCs and can kill the deal.

⚓ **The objective is to get funded.** Talk to your board members, accountant, lawyer, and advisors. You may need to take a lesser value than you initially had in mind. At least you will have funding, which is a lot better than holding on to more equity in a defunct company. There is point where "good enough is good enough." If the company is successful, everyone involved will do well financially.

From The Old Salt's Journal

A startup CEO turned down several VC's that were a few percentage points below his valuation. Money quickly turned tight and he couldn't raise funds at ANY valuation. The company went under.

Another company founder accepted a lower valuation, developed his product and sold the company to a large public company for several hundred millions of dollars.

Remember: Cash is King!

The Business Plan: Creating the Map

After all of our planning, now is the time we put pen to parchment and actually draw out our map. We have all the essential elements of a solid business model in place; it's time to write the business plan. Remember, raising funds is a sales process in that you are selling a part of your company. The VC's are the customers and your business plan is competing against hundreds of plans a VC receives every month. A well-written plan:

- ⚓ Emphasizes the positive aspects of the company and why it will be successful

- ⚓ Invites investors to share in the future success of the company

- ⚓ Focuses on the key essential elements needed to attract investment

The plan should be no more than 40 pages long, including the financial statements. Get suggestions, input and critiques from others, but write the plan yourself. Only you and your fellow founders have the in-depth knowledge and experience to make the plan a true representation of your vision and corporate identity. Your style and substance will separate it from the hundreds of form-structured "cookie cutter" lifeless documents that VC's receive every month.

If you have charted the course to account for the obstacles you may encounter, then the written business plan (the map you draw) is a summary of the model you have developed.

Many people have difficulty in writing their business plans because they have a flawed business model with major obstacles still in their way.

Business Plan Outline

The sections of the plan describe the pieces of the business model you have built:

- ⚓ Cover Page
- ⚓ Table of Contents
- ⚓ Executive Summary
- ⚓ Market Opportunity
- ⚓ Products/Services
- ⚓ Management Team
- ⚓ Financial Statements
- ⚓ Use of Proceeds
- ⚓ Significant Milestones
- ⚓ Exit Strategy
- ⚓ Dilution Schedule

Do not include anything that does not say, "This company will be a winner." Focus your effort on driving home strengths and place them toward the front of the plan, after the Executive Summary.

Now let's look at each item in terms of what information is helpful in influencing investors to want to be a part of this exciting opportunity.

Cover Page

Beginning with the Cover Page, everything; graphs, photos, drawings, printing, should be of high quality. The Cover Page contains company location and contact information:

- ⚓ Company name and address

- ⚓ Name of person to contact regarding the business plan

- ⚓ A distribution control number; used to keep a record of who has a copy

- ⚓ A revision number and date; used to keep a record of updated releases

- ⚓ Optional items
  - o Use heavier paper for cover page
  - o Use multiple colors
  - o Include product picture or drawing

Executive Summary

Although the Executive Summary is next in the Business Plan, after the Table of Contents, we will skip it for now and address it in detail later.

Market Opportunity

The Market Opportunity is often the most important section to investors and has a strong influence on the funding decision. Investors will want to see the market opportunity addressed in four ways:

⚓ **Total Market Available**
Is the market large enough to support multiple companies, and their continued growth into potentially very large corporations?

⚓ **Qualified Market**
If the company executes its plan and meets its milestones, is there enough market potential for the initial product to make the projected revenues and profits?

⚓ **Market Stage and Growth Potential**
Is the timing of the market right for the company to take advantage of a growing market with huge upside potential?

⚓ **Market Entry**
Can the company enter the market and establish a presence under its marketing plan or are there significant barriers that must be overcome?

The Product

You need to sing the praises of the product and avoid getting into too much technical information. Remember, you are selling the sizzle and that's what sells the steak. If, however, any of the product sections is a really strong driver, you may want to emphasize it by separating it out into a major topic:

⚓ **Product description**
What does the product do? Include its features and related benefits to meet customer needs.

⚓ **Product differentiation**
What sets it apart from other products and gives customers reason to select it?

⚓ **Competitive analysis**
Who are the competitors, and how do you compare to them in areas that customers will use in deciding which product they will buy? Such comparison areas could include: product performance, functions and features, price, product availability, vendor reputation, service and support etc.

⚓ **Barriers to market entry**
What are the barriers and are they significant or just a little rough water?

⚓ Strategic Alliances

With whom, and what type of relationship? Include joint development agreements, partnerships, licensing agreements, joint-marketing alliances etc. Are there significant commitments from them? That is, do they have any skin in the relationship?

⚓ Marketing and Sales Strategy

What are the major marketing programs and what are the channels of distribution? Will the major sales emphasis be on direct sales to major accounts? If yes, list the top 6 prospects and any commitments on their part. Or will sales be mainly through OEM's or VAR's?

⚓ Customer Commitment

From Customers, do you have any letters of intent to buy or any feedback that puts your company in a positive light? One direct quote from one high potential customer is worth a 100 market research reports.

From The Old Salt's Journal

An experience I had while working at IBM really helped to drive this last point home. One of my positions was with an Industry Marketing group. For this particular project, I had to get the systems product developers to include product features that customers wanted. I attended meeting after meeting with little accomplished. Then I hit on the idea of letting the customer meet face to face with the developers and tell them what they needed.

So I took a group of developers to several automotive plant sites to see first hand how the products were being used and what new features customers wanted. The response was beyond my expectations. The developers not only agreed to add the features that the customers requested, they went back and convinced their management to change the development schedule to prioritize making the features available ahead of other projects.

The Management Team

Here is your chance to toot your own horn. As Donald Trump says, "to be recognized, you must promote yourself, no one else is going to do it for you." Include a paragraph on each key team member. Highlight their personal strengths, experience, expertise, and especially their accomplishments. Investors want to know that your team members, in addition to being very talented, have contributed to the success of other companies in the past. This is a particularly important point investors want to see as part of the CEO's biography.

Also include a paragraph on each board member, highlighting their particular skills and experience that will compliment and help support the management team. Include the advisory board, if there is one, and briefly describe how they will be used. Finally, mention the law and accounting firms and any other professional services involved.

Financials

As we described earlier, you should have created three sets, (best case, worst case and most likely case) of financial statements projected out over the next three years:

- ⚓ Net Income Statement

- ⚓ Cash Flow Statement

- ⚓ Balance Sheet

If the business is up and running and you have actual financials, include them. The numbers should be projected by month for the first year and by quarter for the following two years. The investors will have many questions to gain better insight as to the financial potential of their investment. Be prepared to discuss the details and the assumptions made. Using reasonable assumptions is a critical point. If the investors do not believe the assumptions are realistic, then they will discount much of your forecast and your credibility will take a hit.

The investors will analyze the financial information and ask probing questions to uncover several key bits of information:

- ⚓ When will significant amounts of cash be needed and for what?

- ⚓ What is the burn rate and what events will have the most effect on it?

- ⚓ When will the company turn profitable? What assumptions are involved?

- ⚓ Will the company still be able to survive under the worst case scenario?

- ⚓ Are the projections realistic or are they "blue sky"?

- ⚓ What happens to the financials if the assumptions are adjusted to a more conservative level?

Remember, the financials must present a view of a well thought-out business model that is do-able and shows potential for significant financial gains.

Use of Proceeds

Investors want to know what the money will be used for, how much is needed, and when it will be needed. The best approach is to present a table of functions and milestones the money will be used for, the amount needed, and the date it will be needed. Example functions:

- ⚓ Human Resources:
  Salaries, benefits, recruiting

- ⚓ Facilities:
  Leases, renovation, furnishings

- ⚓ Product Development (R&D):
  Equipment, software

- ⚓ Sales & Marketing:
  Product launch, building sales channels, start up of web site

- ⚓ Professional Services:
  Legal, accounting, consultants

- ⚓ Product Manufacturing:
  Ramp-up

Exit Strategy

This is a critical topic for investors that is often overlooked or given minimal thought by the founders. Investors want to know how they are going to make money on this investment and when. They are not investing for the long haul. Their mode of operation is to invest, support the startup and initial growth phases, and cash out. The two most basic exit strategies are:

- ⚓ Take the company public (IPO) and the investors can sell their ownership share in the company.

- ⚓ Sell the company, usually to another company.

You will have to describe the exit strategy and the target date. If you plan to sell the company, list several companies that could be potential buyers.

Dilution Summary

List all of ownership shares and percentage of equity, including what the investors will own. Include common stock, preferred convertible, warrants, and employee stock option plans. The equity ownership must total 100%.

Appendices

Include any information that shows the
company in a positive light. Examples:

- Market Research Data

- Trade Press Articles

- Customer Testimonials

- Key Employee Resumes

- References to Technical White Papers

- Intellectual Property Information

- Product Flyers. Promotional Pieces

- Summary of Alliance or Licensing
  Agreements

The Executive Summary in Depth

Although the Executive Summary is included in the front of the business plan, we are giving it more attention as a stand-alone document because of its importance to the funding process. VC's will take the time to read a two to three page Executive Summary, and based on its impact may, or as in most cases may not, look at the business plan. In other words, the Executive Summary is the most important document you need to produce. You will use it whenever people ask you for a brief description of your business. It creates the first, and sometimes only, impression of you and your business.

The first paragraph of the Executive Summary is the most important.   If it does not peak the interest of the VC, the VC will not review the rest of the summary, let alone the business plan.

Begin with a brief line or two describing who you are and what your business is. Then describe how and why you will be successful in the market. Remember, this is a selling process and the Executive Summary can be thought of as a sales promotion piece that has the objective of getting the VC interested enough to read the business plan and become aware of the potential rewards in being associated with your company.

Now address each of the major sections of the business plan highlighting the strongest points in each section:

⚓ Market Opportunity

⚓ Products/Services

⚓ Management Team

⚓ Financial Statements

⚓ Use of Proceeds

⚓ Exit Strategy

Market Opportunity

Make the point that the qualified market addressed is large enough to support the projected growth of the company and the overall market offers the opportunity for future products.

Products/Services

Be sure to describe what need or customer problem the product addresses. Highlight product differentiation and advantages over the competition. Focus attention on any alliances, joint ventures or actual customer commitments to buy the product.

Management Team

Although you must have the complete package in terms of a business model, the people who will run the company are still a primary investment factor. Drive home the capabilities, experience and accomplishments of the key members of the team.

Financials

Use a summary of the "most likely case" of three-year financial projections. Show how much you have already raised, and how much cash you will need to support the business plan. Emphasize your Plan to Profitability showing when the business will turn cash flow positive.

Use of Proceeds

Highlight the major uses of the money and when they will occur. Make sure you can account for where most of the money will be used and that there isn't a large difference between the total amount being raised and the total amount identified for specific uses.

Exit Strategy

Describe your exit strategy and the timeframe. Even if planning an IPO, mention the type of companies that should have an interest in buying the company.

Executive Summary Gold Nuggets:

⚓ Try to create a positive, optimistic, confidence in success, high potential, image of the company by focusing on the strongest attributes.

⚓ Avoid lengthy product descriptions and technical details. Rather, zero in on the key product differentiators.

⚓ Show that you have a Plan to Profitability within a reasonable time frame.

⚓ Keep it as brief as possible: Three pages maximum.

Now your map is complete, except for the determining the exact destination.   It's time to figure out exactly where to draw that "X" on your map.

Part 4
Choosing Your Destination

At
this point you must look for the right island and figure out the best place to dig for your treasure. Pick an island that has the correct resources to make your trip worthwhile.

Connecting With The Right Venture Capitalist

Just as you defined the market for your product, now it's time to define the market for your company. Remember, in this case, the VC's are the buyers, and you are selling them a portion of your company. So with hundreds of VC's out there, how do we find the ones with the highest potential of investing in your company?

First, VCs are becoming more and more specialized. Their investment priorities may be:

⚓ **By Industry**
high technology, biotech,
consumer products, etc.

⚓ **By Location**
Silicon Valley, Midwest,
Northeast, Southeast, International

⚓ **By Investment Stage**
seed, startup, later stage

⚓ **By Investment Size**
up to $2 million, from
$5 million to $15 million, etc.

Second, when it comes to VC's willing to step up and commit funds, there are "Followers" and there are "Leaders." Many VC's would rather have another VC take the lead in an investment. Working with follower VC types can be very time consuming and a drain on your limited resources. They never say "no", but continue to string you along to see if you can attract a quality lead investor.

From The Old Salt's Journal

We were brought into a situation where a VC had been in discussions with the founders for about a year without investing. The founders said the VC knew everything there was to know about the company but would not make a decision. We brought in a new VC, who was known to take the lead position, and within 6 weeks the funding was in place. The original VC never did invest.

Looking for Places to Dig

So how do you look for VC's and find out about their investment criteria? There are industry publications and many sources on-line. Some are free; others charge a fee to access their list. Many ask you for your fund raising 'criteria' and then charge you for each name (and their contact information) that meets your criteria.

National Venture Capital Association

http://www.nvca.org/
Lists Venture Capital firms and their specialties.

Business.com

http://www.business.com/directory/financial_servic es/venture_capital/firms_and_funds/
Refers to itself 'The Business Search Engine'" and lists VC information in the "Venture Capital Firms and Funds" area of its site.

Vfinance.com

http://www.vfinance.com/
Charges fee per name that matches your criteria

X Marks the Spot

Once you have several VC Firm names, do some research by visiting their web sites. Most of them post the information you are looking for:

⚓ Industries they invest in

⚓ Investment criteria

⚓ Stage of investments

⚓ Geographic preferences

⚓ Size of investments

⚓ List of investments

⚓ Biography of each VC

You should find about six VC firms whose investment profiles you match. Try to identify the particular VC (person) within each firm who has made investments in companies similar to yours.

Contact CEO's of their portfolio companies and talk to them about their experience with this VC. Be sure to ask what it was about their company that convinced the VC to make an investment. Once you have done your homework, it's time to make contact.

When you contact the VC's you must share enough information to generate interest in your company. Some entrepreneurs are concerned about giving the VC's too much of their sensitive information in that it may somehow be distributed to others. They may try to protect themselves by asking the VC's to sign a non-disclosure agreement or "NDA." NDA's are commonly used to protect the confidential information that often must be shared between companies when they work together.

Very few VC's will agree to sign an NDA. Usually the terms must be negotiated and that takes time and legal support. You do not need to worry about VC's stealing your ideas. They live and die by their reputations in the investment community. Also, their business is to invest and support the future growth and success of your ideas, not to create their own version of your company.

From The Old Salt's Journal

Many years ago, a VC asked me to accompany him on a visit to an entrepreneur who had a demonstration for a new software product. During the meeting, we saw a limited demonstration, but the individual was very concerned about sharing any of the details of his product. He wanted an NDA that his lawyer had drafted that contained terms and conditions that were difficult for any VC to accept. The result was that this VC, as well as several others, liked the basic idea that was demonstrated, but no one would sign the NDA. The company never got funded. The idea was a software search engine used to search for information on the Internet.

You can contact VC's in several ways:

⚓ You can send them your business plan with a personalized cover letter. Unfortunately, the better VC firms receive hundreds of unsolicited business plans every month. There is a slight chance that an associate will look at the Executive Summary and follow-up with you.

⚓ You can send a personalized e-mail with the Executive Summary attached, directly to the targeted VC. This is why the Executive Summary is a critical document. If it wows the VC, there's some chance of follow-up.

⚓ You can be personally referred to the VC. This approach by far, is the best way to get a VC to consider investing in your company.

Being personally recommended by someone the VC respects and relates to, gives you a big advantage over the pile of unsolicited business plans. You now have instant credibility because the VC knows the person recommending you would not risk their reputation and relationship if they weren't convinced that this is an opportunity worth consideration.

How do you get someone to refer you? You may have mutual friends or business associates that know the VC. You may have contacts within one of the companies in the VC investment portfolio. You could have gone to the same school or belong to the same professional societies or associations.

If you need a professional referral, there are companies such as ours, Venture Capital Strategies, that can help to get you in front of the right VC's and help you prepare to make a "deal closing" presentation.

A word of caution when working with companies to gain access to VC's. Be very leery if they ask for up-front fees. It is reasonable to pay them a small percentage of the money raised, but only if you obtain funding.

**Now that you know where you're going, it's
time to put the boat into the water
and start your voyage!**

Part 5
Setting Sail is Setting "Sale"

Ready to set sail? You've prepared yourself well and know how to avoid major obstacles on the sea. Test the wind, set your sails, and get underway. Anticipate smooth sailing.

The VC "Sales" Presentation

Successful Sailing requires "Sale-ing." We call it a "sales" presentation because that's exactly what it is. When you visit a VC's office, most likely you will be ushered into one of several conference rooms. You may notice that there are meetings and presentations going on in the other rooms. VC's sit through a large number of presentations from companies like yours every day and yet they invest in a very small percentage of them. So your challenge is to get the VC excited and convinced that your company represents a better investment opportunity than all others, and then to take positive action.

The presentation itself, should take about 20 to 30 minutes, and expect the VC's to ask a lot of questions adding another 30 minutes to an hour. Your presentation should center around10 to 15 high quality slides. Each slide should be in bullet form with key points to talk to, and concept drawings should be as simplistic as possible. It's not the quantity of the visuals, it's more their ability to convey your message that is important.

From The Old Salt's Journal

I was involved with a group that was promoting a new manufacturing process. We invited 25 editors of industry publications to a seminar in hopes of getting some of them interested enough to write positive articles. One product manager had over 90 slides.

Half way through his 90-minute presentation, he asked if there were any questions. One very prominent editor spoke up and said he was totally confused and lost.

The next presenter had only one concept slide that he used to educate the group on the basics of the new process. His presentation was 20 minutes, but he created enough interest and excitement that the Q&A session went on for another 45 minutes. Not only did he get eight of the editors to publish articles, but one of them also used his slide as the cover of the next issue of the magazine.

Why did they respond so positively to him? There were several reasons. One, he took the time to find out the level of knowledge most of his audience had on the subject and used it as a base to teach them about the new process. Second, he was calmly enthusiastic and confident. Third, he answered all their questions and addressed their concerns with a positive attitude. In other words, he sold them.

VC's expect you to, and indeed you must cover the major topics of your business model:

- ⚓ Market Opportunity

- ⚓ Product

- ⚓ Management Team

- ⚓ Financials

- ⚓ Use of Proceeds

- ⚓ Exit Strategy

- ⚓ Dilution Summary

They will be looking at each of these areas to see if there are any of the obstacles that we have discussed earlier in this book. Given you have a solid plan; they now want to be "SOLD" on you and your plan.

Remember when we were talking about Product Differentiation in our discussion about your Cargo? Our VC friend asked us about the "hook" that made our product unique and set it high above the competition.

The same principle applies to your VC presentation. Just as your product needs a 'hook' to set it apart, so does your presentation. Now is the time to catch and reel in that VC.

<u>Your Voyage</u>

The "hook" is made up of several elements that can send you off on a successful **VOYAGE.**

V	**VISION**	Demonstrate a clear understanding of where you want to take the company
O	**OPPORTUNITY**	Show that there is a large potential market for this product
Y	**YEARNING**	The desire, dedication and passion to build a successful company
A	**ABILITY**	An experienced management team with a successful track record
G	**GAME PLAN**	A solid and do-able business plan
E	**ENTHUSIASM**	A strong, confident, positive attitude and a sense of urgency to succeed

These are the traits that separate the average presentation from a winning one. One strong word of caution: You must be yourself. Don't try to portray yourself as having different personality traits than you really have. People will see through it. If you are very low key, you may want to present the topics that you are strongest in and have another member (or members) of the team do a larger portion of the presentation. Keep in mind that you may be working with this group of VC's for several years, and there might be periods of rough seas to navigate. To have a safe trip requires the crew and the investors to work together in an atmosphere of total trust and commitment.

If the presentation goes well, and you have "hooked" the VC, you may be asked back to meet with other partners or associates, or you may soon be handed the key to the treasure chest, the term sheet.

Part 6
The Term Sheet:
Key to the Treasure Chest

Congratulations, you have separated from the pack. The VC has presented you with a document that expresses an interest in investing in your company. It is usually a term sheet, but may be a letter of intent or an investment memorandum.

They all serve the same function, which is to state an expressed interest but not to form a binding commitment. Basically, the document represents the amount they are willing to invest and under what terms, assuming their due diligence agrees with the scenario that you presented to them.

Some of the terms and conditions are standard, and some can be negotiated. If you do not have prior experience with term sheets, and even if you do, this is the time to invest in a well-respected lawyer that has experience in this area. A good lawyer can review the document and tell you if this is a reasonable offer and:

⚓ What points are non-negotiable

⚓ What points are in your interest to negotiate for better terms

⚓ What points are in your interest to eliminate

A top notch lawyer may have dealt with this particular VC firm before, and will know what points to leverage, and what points may kill the deal. Unfortunately, well over half the term sheets presented, do not end up in closing funding. Also, most term sheets contain a clause stating that you are responsible for all legal fees and expenses, including the VC's, even if the deal is cancelled. This can add up to $20,000 to $50,000.

Before you sign, here are some of the most important points to consider:

Funding

⚓ **Valuation**

Is it what you expected? If not, you can still negotiate.

⚓ **Amount to be Invested**

Is it the full amount you need? If not, who will raise the rest of it?

⚓ **Funds Availability**

Is the full amount available up front or in multiple releases (tranches)? Staged releases are usually tied to milestones. Are the milestones reasonable? If a milestone is missed, what are the possible effects on the amount of funds and on the terms and conditions?

Terms and Conditions

⚓ How many Board seats will the VC's get and how many will the founders get? What are the voting rights? Will the VC's control the Board?

⚓ Is there an <u>anti-dilution clause</u>? If so, is it a "ratcheting" or "weighted averaging" provision? In ratcheting, if you later need to raise funds and must do so at lower valuation, the VC's price per share is lowered (ratcheted down) to take advantage of the lower valuation. You should try to avoid a ratcheting clause. With weighted averaging, the VC's position is adjusted in proportion to the new, lower valuation.

⚓ Is there a <u>standstill clause</u>? This means you cannot do any fund raising activities or seek other investors until the funding closes or the VC's decide not to fund. An open-ended standstill clause should be avoided. It puts you in limbo and at the mercy of the VC's to get their due diligence done. Your market value, your fund raising momentum, and your working capital could all take a serious hit if the VC's drag out the due diligence process. If you can't eliminate this clause, try to negotiate a time limit that will motivate the VC's to close or move on.

⚓ Are there any terms or conditions that you had discussed and agreed to with the VC's, which are not included in the term sheet? If so, clear them up before you sign the term sheet and the final documents are drawn.

Once you have negotiated and are completely comfortable with all the terms; then and only then, should you sign the term sheet. Once you sign, you have a business deal. You and the VC's will get one last chance to alter or kill the deal when the final documents are presented. But first, there is one remaining obstacle to address, and that is the due diligence process.

Land Ho! You can see the shoreline now. The journey is almost complete, but before you can drop anchor, your navigation skills will be tested one more time.

Part 7
Due Diligence:
Walking the Plank

Now that you have agreed on the terms and signed the term sheet, there's one final obstacle to surmount before you break out the champagne and celebrate: that is "Due Diligence".

Due Diligence is the process in which the VC examines the investment opportunity in greater detail to verify and confirm that what you have presented is accurate and reasonable and/or to uncover any problems that may exist.

To do so, the VC will usually look at these areas:

To do so, the VC will usually look at these areas:

Documentation

They will want to see every piece of documentation in existence; Particularly, all financial information, legal issues, contracts and agreements. To save some time, gather the documents into indexed binders.

Business Fundamentals

They will drill down on the major areas of the business model:

⚓ The People

They will check backgrounds and assess their capabilities. It is a wise move to disclose any potential background problems. The VC's will check your personal history as well as your business career. They will check with their own industry contacts as well as with your references.

⚓ The Market

They will conduct their own market analysis and compare it to yours. The VC may contact your customers, suppliers, business alliances and current investors. You should contact them in advance and let them know they may get a call from the VC. During these discussions, the VC's will also be testing to see if your marketing and sales strategies are on target.

⚓ **The Product**
They may use consultants to evaluate the potential "added value" and development feasibility of your products. The VC's want to verify that your products are competitively viable and there is a substantial growth market for them.

⚓ **The Financials**
They will make their own forecast of burn rate and cash requirements. They will use the worse case scenario to test and see if the company could still survive. They will insist that the financials be auditable.

Site Visit

They will want to visit your site to talk to people and get a feel as to the workplace atmosphere. They will be particularly interested in talking to the key people to gauge their commitment to staying with the company and supporting the management team.

The Due Diligence process usually takes about 30 days. Based on the outcome, the VC's will make their decision. If they decide to fund, be aware, they usually find some problem areas and may use them as reasons to change the terms and/or valuation. Make sure you are in complete agreement before the closing documents are prepared. You may need to do some additional negotiating, but always remember the objective is to get funded, and until the closing documents are signed, the coins are still locked up in the VC's treasure chest.

Once you have completed Due Diligence, you have arrived at Venture Capital Funding Island. Drop your Anchor! Then go open your Treasure Chest.

Part 8
You Have Arrived!

Congratulations, your ship has landed safely at VC Funding Island and you have found the treasure chest.

The Treasure

Once the VC's have come to agreement with you on the final terms and valuation, they will prepare a set of closing documents. It will contain a stock purchase agreement, employment agreement, and corporate documents. Most of the provisions in the documents are standard or "boiler plate". Your lawyer can explain them to you and alert you to any provisions that are different from (or in addition to) your understanding of the terms of the deal. Read the documents carefully. Once you sign, the terms are binding and the funds are made available. You have succeeded! Put these gold coins to good use and they will multiply your riches.

A Few Words from The Old Salt

Although during the voyage there are sometimes rough waters, and many boats fall to the bottom of the sea, the true entrepreneur will find a way to survive. If you are that person, you will meet and beat the challenges and obstacles and sail on to find funding. You will have no doubt that the work and commitment were well worth the trip. One last word of counsel, now that you have the coins, put them to use wisely. You never know if you will find another treasure chest.

Part 9
Ship's Log

Summary of
Obstacles & Sailing Tips

	Obstacles	For Smooth Sailing
1	**Insufficient Personal Commitment in Terms of Personal Time, Money and Dedication**	Make The Personal Commitment in Time, Money, and Dedication
2	**Lack of Experienced Management**	Hire Experienced Managers with Solid Credentials
3	**A Weak or Inexperienced CEO**	Find a Strong CEO who VC's can Work with and is Adaptable and Flexible

4	Size of the Qualified Market	Large Qualified Market, Early Growth Stage, Upward Trend
5	Not enough Product Differentiation	Develop Products with "Added Value" Differentiation that Addresses Customer Needs and Market Trends
6	Weak Competitive Position	Use presentation methods and models that show your product in the best competitive light
7	Low Barriers to Market Entry	Protect your position and technology. Create exclusive relationships and Patent. Patent. Patent.

8	No early Market Acceptance	Signal support of your product to investors by securing statements from customers or credible allies
9	Many Barriers to Market Acceptance	Modify product to remove or neutralize barriers and 'sell-around' them.
10	Too Few Strategic Alliances	Create high quality and mutually beneficial relationships with strategic companies
11	Weak marketing and sales strategy	Develop Strong Marketing and Sales Plans that Target Key Customers
12	Burn Rate Increasing over a period of 3 years	Conserve Cash. Spend only on necessary and timely business activities

13	Long Path to Profitability	Shorten Path to Profitability by tightly managing cash flow; focusing on early revenue generation and early market entry.
14	Poor Scalability	Conserve cash so business can grow rapidly without draining funds. Adjust market placement and/or product differentiation to increase growth rate

INDEX

About the Authors

Ronald J. Carlini:

Ron has held several executive and senior management positions in the semiconductor and telecommunications industries.

Mr. Carlini played a major role in the negotiations and in the due diligence process that resulted in Amati Communications being acquired by Texas Instruments Inc. for $398 million.

During his career, Mr. Carlini has developed an extensive network of contacts with venture capitalists, industry analysts, investment bankers, and law firms that specialize in new business ventures. He has helped raise investment funds for over 20 companies.

Therese Carlini Moss:

Therese has worked in the high tech industry for 20 years. She has held executive management positions at both start-up companies and major high tech corporations. Her industry experience includes consumer and business-to-business e-commerce. Therese earned an MBA from Santa Clara University.

About VCS

Venture Capital Strategies was founded to address the need of companies to be better prepared, in today's difficult economic climate, for raising operating capital and for forming strategic alliances.

Entrepreneurs:

Venture Capitalists have raised their requirements for funding. *Venture Capital Strategies* helps entrepreneurs to identify and meet today's more vigorous requirements by providing the tools, techniques, and methodologies that help both investors and entrepreneurs through the funding process more quickly and with less pain. Venture Capital Strategies can help your company improve your chances of obtaining venture capital.

Mergers and Alliances:

Venture Capital Strategies helps companies find strategic partners and creative funding alternatives. Through developing a customized solution for your company's situation and needs, leveraging: our investor and VC network, hands-on team coaching, customized tools, Venture Capital Strategies can help your company successfully locate and engage a strong synergistic partner.

Investors:

Venture Capital Strategies works with only selected, highly qualified companies. Prior to introducing them to investors, we assist companies in developing their business model, focusing in the areas of: Market Potential, Financials, Management, Product, and Strategic Alliances. *Venture Capital Strategies* can help investors find investment opportunities that meet their individual investment criteria.

Contact VCS:

www.venturecapitalstrategies.com
Telephone: (408) 278-7062

Attention colleges and universities, Corporations, and Entrepreneur clubs and Organizations: Quantity discounts are available on bulk purchases of this book for educational training purposes, fund-raising, or gift giving. Special books, booklets, or book excerpts can also be created to fit your specific needs.

For Information contact Venture Capital Strategies at: www.venturecapitalstrategies.com or send email to bookorders@venturecapitalstrategies.com

Our team is also available to conduct half-day seminars and workshops.

Quick Order Form

Internet Orders: www.venturecapitalstrategies.com

E-mail Orders: Orders@venturecapitalstrategies.com

Phone Orders: 408-278-7062

Postal Orders: Venture Capital Strategies
1685 Branham Lane, Suite 270
San Jose, CA 95118

Smooth Sailing To Venture Capital Funding
By Ron Carlini and Therese Carlini Moss

# of books @ 19.95 each	
# of books on CD @19.95 each	
Merchandise Sub-total	
7.75% sales tax (CA residents only)	
Shipping and Handling	
Total Enclosed	

Shipping and Handling:

US: $4.00 for first book or disk and $2.00 for each additional product.

International: $9.00 for first book or disk and $5.00 for each additional product

Name	
Address	
City	
State and Zip	
Email	
Phone	
Charge To:	□ Check Enclosed □Visa □MasterCard □ AMEX
Card Number Expiration Date	
Name on Card	
Authorized Signature	

□ Yes, Add me to your e-mail and mailings of VCS Offerings, Seminars, and Publications